E.S.L. Support Centre,
Hadley Juniors,
Crescent Road,
Hadley.

SMDS
MADELEY COURT SCHOOL
COURT STREET, MADELEY
TELFORD TF7 5DZ
Telephone: 585704

S M D S
HOLLINSWOOD
JUNIORS

S M D S
HOLLINSWOOD
JUNIORS

Religious Stories

Guru Nanak and the Sikh Gurus

Ranjit Arora

Illustrated by
Iain MacLeod-Brudenell

Wayland

Religious Stories

Buddhist Stories
Chinese Stories
Creation Stories
Guru Nanak and the Sikh Gurus
Hindu Stories
The Life of the Buddha
The Life of Jesus
The Life of Muhammad
The Lives of the Saints
Old Testament Stories

Edited by: Jillie Norrey

First published in 1987 by
Wayland Publishers Ltd
61 Western Road, Hove,
East Sussex BN3 1JD, England

© Copyright 1987 Wayland (Publishers) Ltd

British Library Cataloguing in Publication Data
Arora, R. K.
　Guru Nanak and the Sikh gurus. – (Religious stories)
　1. Sikhism – Juvenile literature
　I. Title　　II. MacLeod-Brudenell, Iain
　III. Series
　294.6　　　BL2018

ISBN 0 85078 906 0

Phototypeset by
Kalligraphics Ltd, Redhill, Surrey
Printed in Italy by
G. Canale & C.Sp.A., Turin
Bound in the U.K. by
The Bath Press, Avon

Contents

The story of Makkah   8

The banquet of Malak Bhago   18

A lesson in humility   26

What makes a true Guru   38

The creation of the *Khalsa*   48

Glossary   60

Textual note   61

Books to read   62

8

The story of Makkah

Long ago there lived a holy man called Guru Nanak who had a friend called Mardana. They used to travel together from place to place, singing in praise of God.

Once Guru Nanak and Mardana visited a place called Makkah. Muslims from all over the world come to pray at the big mosque there because it is their holy city.

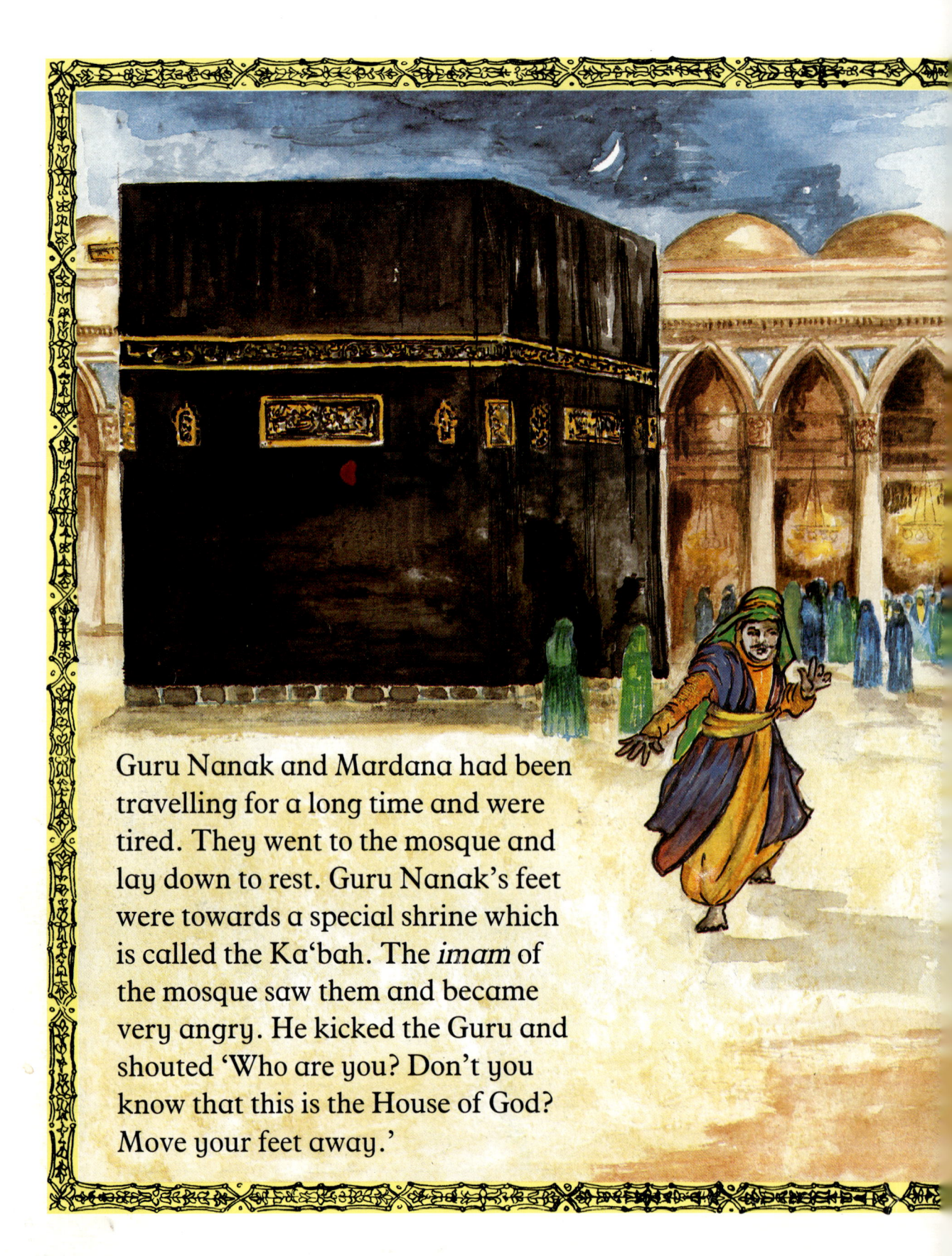

Guru Nanak and Mardana had been travelling for a long time and were tired. They went to the mosque and lay down to rest. Guru Nanak's feet were towards a special shrine which is called the Ka'bah. The *imam* of the mosque saw them and became very angry. He kicked the Guru and shouted 'Who are you? Don't you know that this is the House of God? Move your feet away.'

11

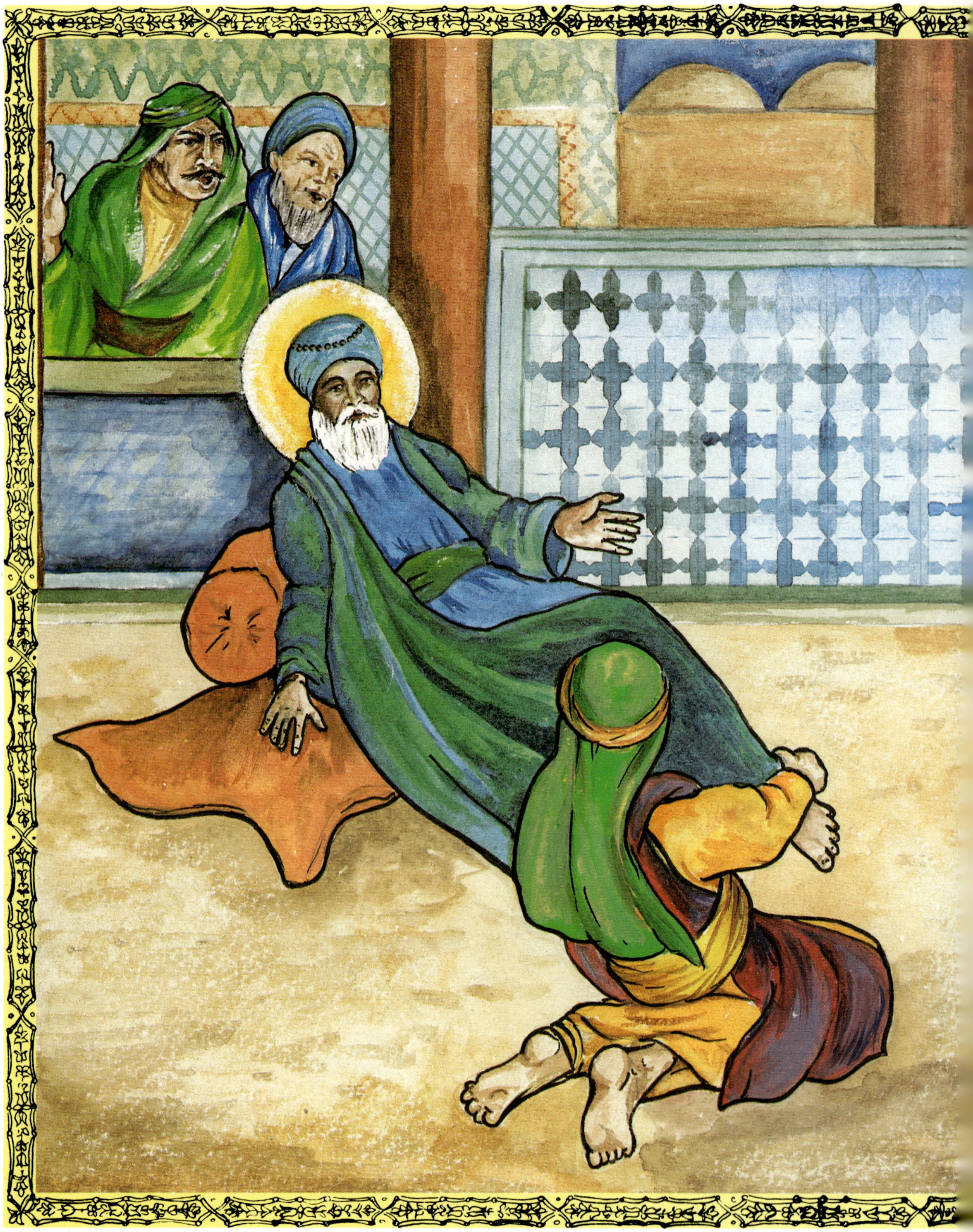

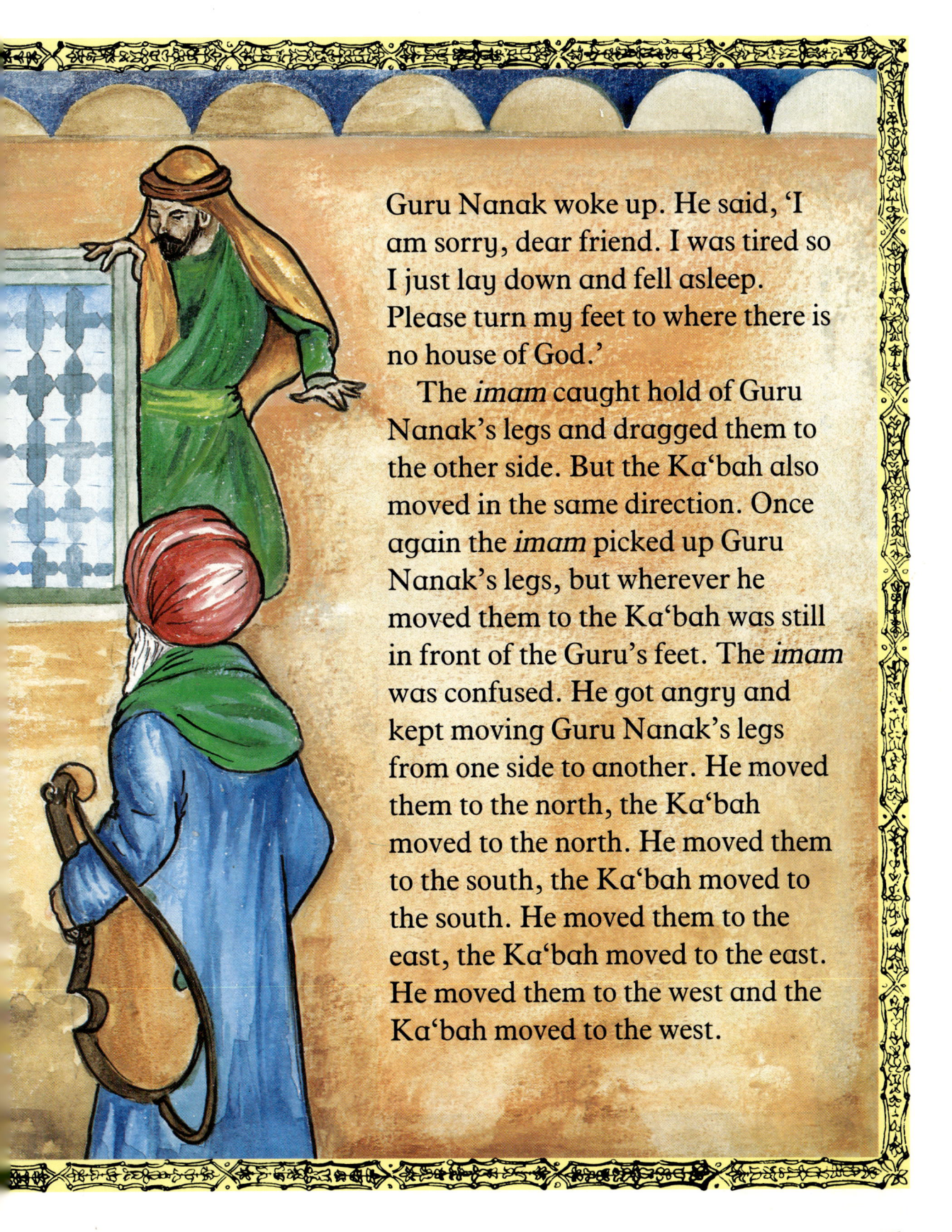

Guru Nanak woke up. He said, 'I am sorry, dear friend. I was tired so I just lay down and fell asleep. Please turn my feet to where there is no house of God.'

The *imam* caught hold of Guru Nanak's legs and dragged them to the other side. But the Ka'bah also moved in the same direction. Once again the *imam* picked up Guru Nanak's legs, but wherever he moved them to the Ka'bah was still in front of the Guru's feet. The *imam* was confused. He got angry and kept moving Guru Nanak's legs from one side to another. He moved them to the north, the Ka'bah moved to the north. He moved them to the south, the Ka'bah moved to the south. He moved them to the east, the Ka'bah moved to the east. He moved them to the west and the Ka'bah moved to the west.

14

The *imam* was so upset, he could not speak. A crowd of people gathered around them. Everyone was surprised. No-one could understand what was happening.

Guru Nanak said, 'Listen to me, my friend. God does not live in one place. He lives everywhere. He lives in every one of you.' Guru Nanak then said to his friend, 'Dear Mardana, let us sing.'

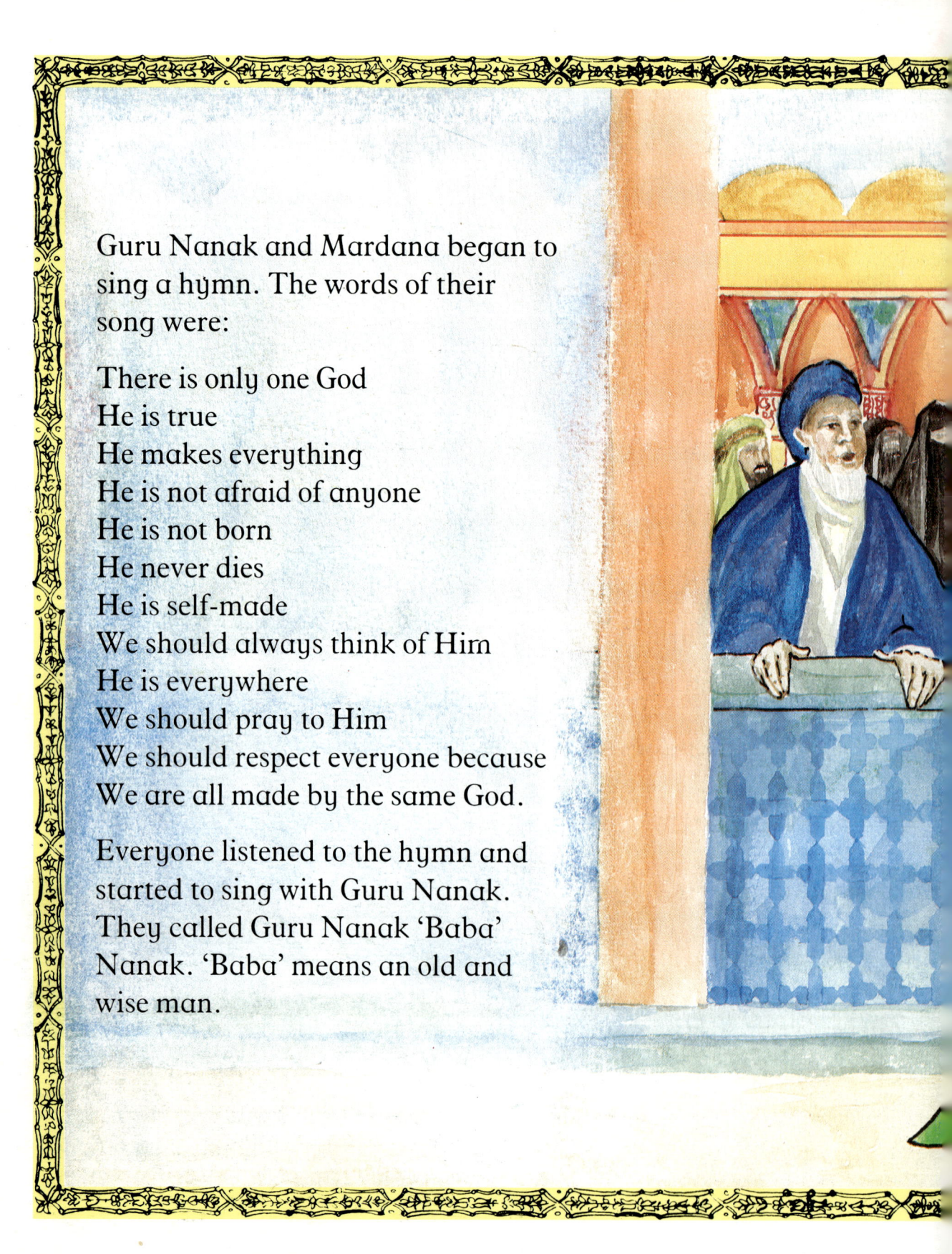

Guru Nanak and Mardana began to sing a hymn. The words of their song were:

There is only one God
He is true
He makes everything
He is not afraid of anyone
He is not born
He never dies
He is self-made
We should always think of Him
He is everywhere
We should pray to Him
We should respect everyone because
We are all made by the same God.

Everyone listened to the hymn and started to sing with Guru Nanak. They called Guru Nanak 'Baba' Nanak. 'Baba' means an old and wise man.

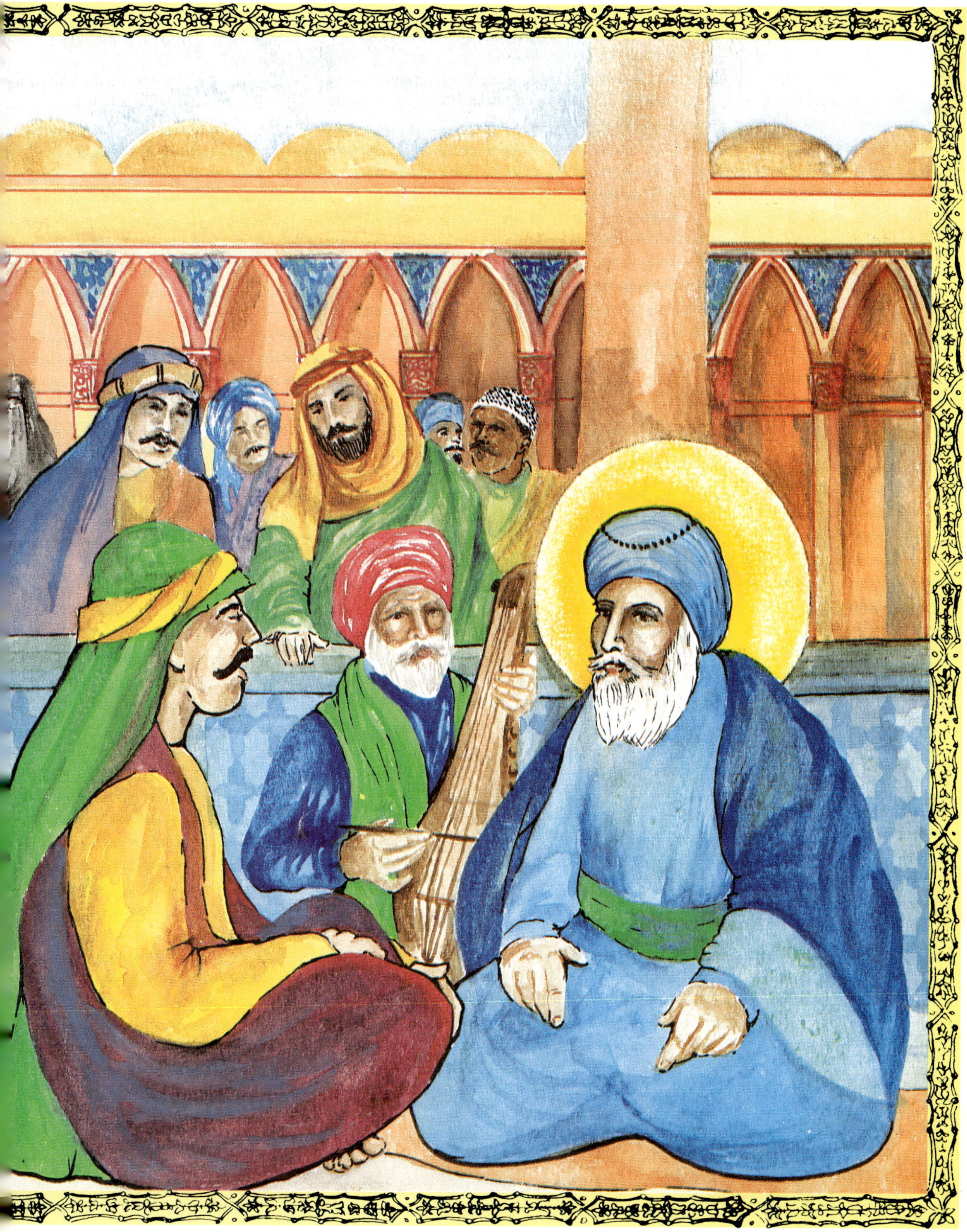

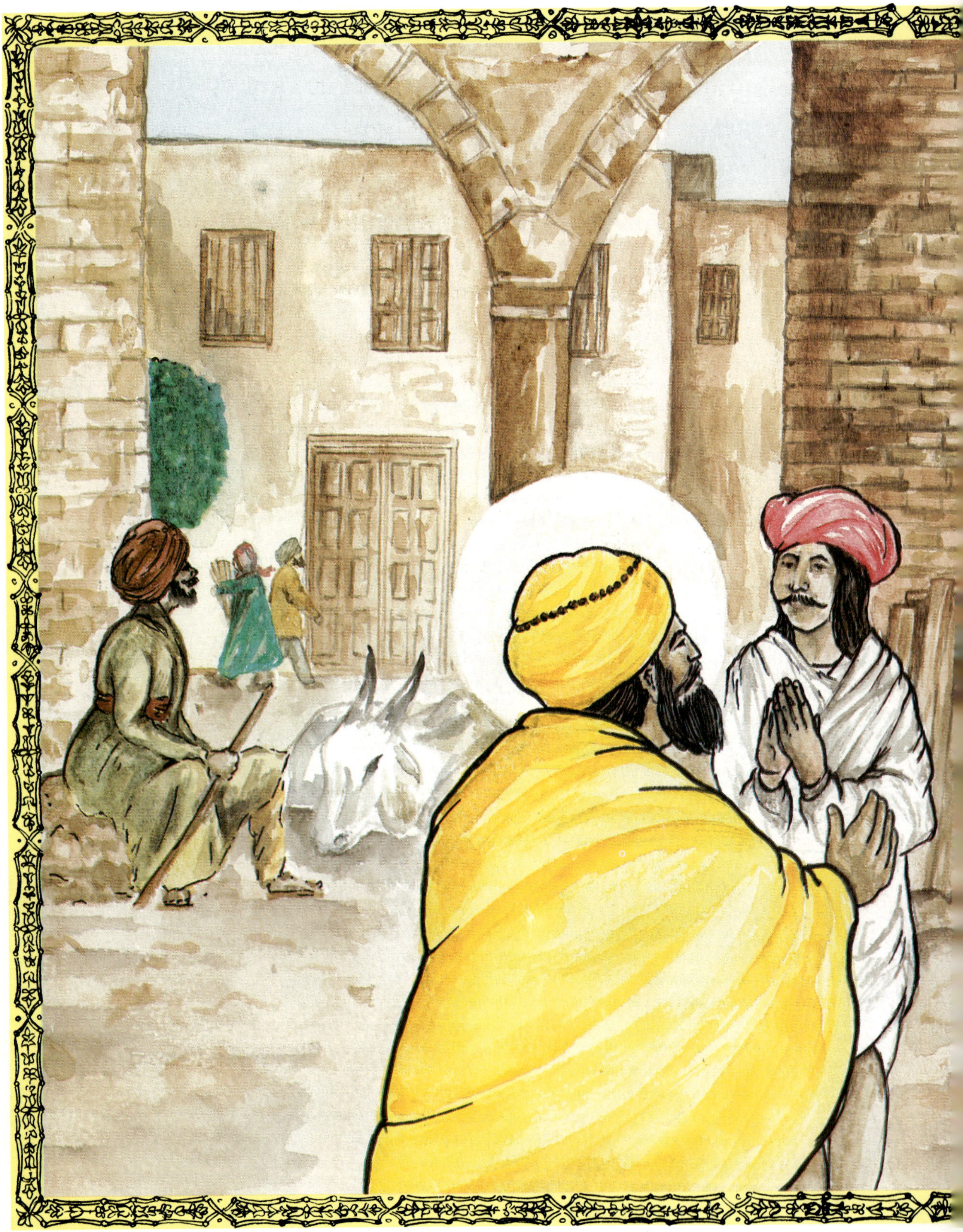

The banquet of Malak Bhago

Guru Nanak and Mardana visited a town called Aimenabad where there lived a poor carpenter called Lalo. When Lalo met Guru Nanak and his friend he welcomed them and gave them simple food to eat.

20

Guru Nanak stayed at Lalo's house for a few days. Every morning and evening Guru Nanak and his friend sang hymns and said prayers. When people came to Lalo's house, Guru Nanak would tell them 'There is only one God. Truth is His name. You should live a good life. You should work hard and earn an honest living.'

In the same town lived a man called Malak Bhago. He was very rich and he worked for a powerful businessman.

Malak Bhago planned a banquet and invited the town's famous and rich people to dinner. Guru Nanak refused the invitation he was sent, preferring to stay with Lalo.

Malak Bhago was not very happy. He sent for Guru Nanak and said to him, 'You eat dinner with a man who is neither rich nor famous and you refuse my invitation. Please tell me, why don't you like my food?'

Guru Nanak said, 'Dear friend, I'll show you why I don't want to eat your food. Please bring me the *kachori* that is now being cooked in your kitchen.'

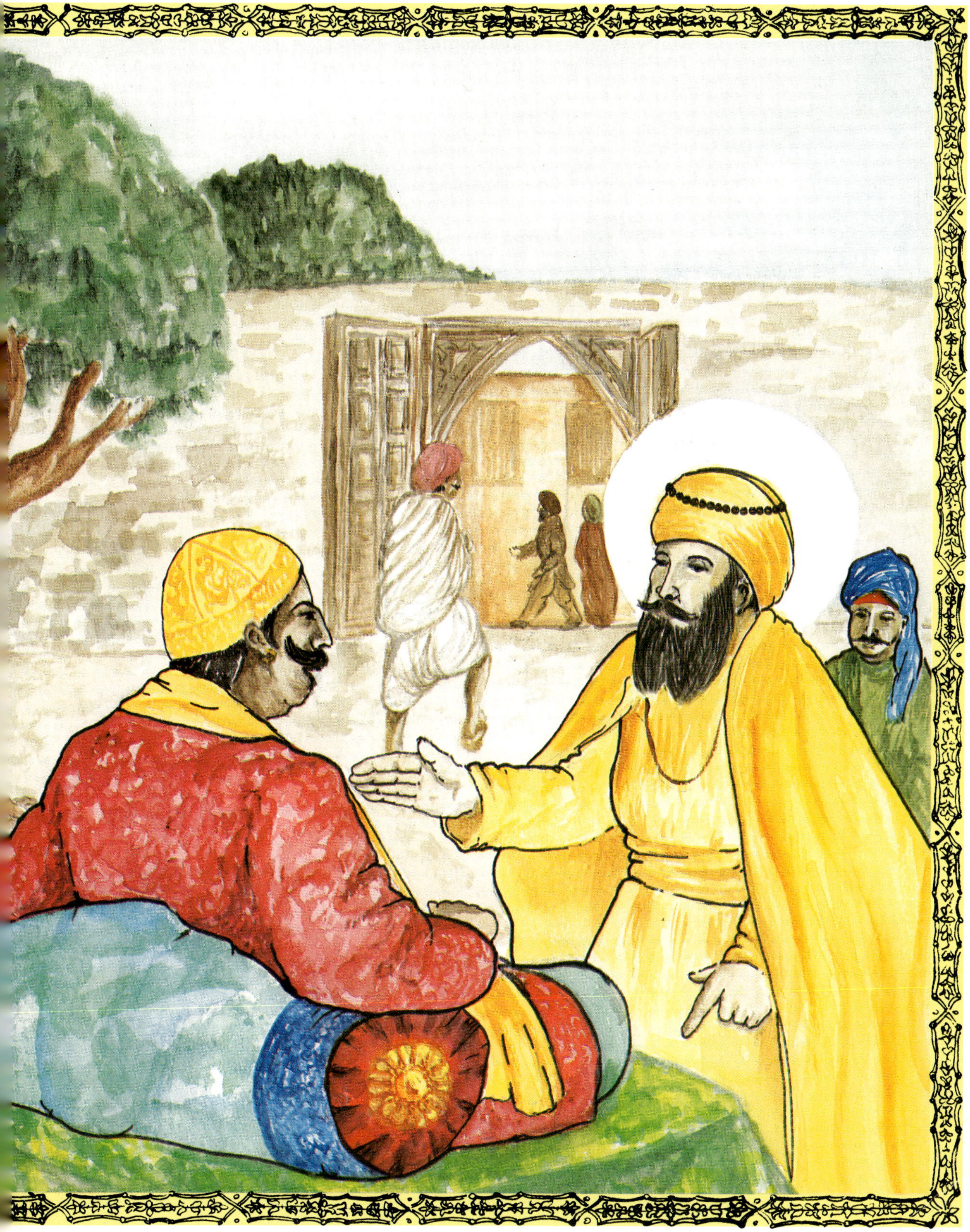

Guru Nanak then said to his friend, 'Please bring me the *roti* which is being cooked in Lalo's kitchen at this moment.'

Guru Nanak then got hold of the *kachori* in one hand and the *roti* in another hand. He squeezed them both. People were shocked to see that there was blood dripping from one hand and milk dripping from the other.

Guru Nanak then said to Malak Bhago, 'Dear friend, now can you see milk dripping from Lalo's *roti* and blood dripping from your *kachori*? Lalo's *roti* is bought with money earned from hard work and honest living. Your *kachoris* taste very nice but are full of blood. They are not bought with your honest money but with money you robbed from other people.'

Everyone was astonished. But they were all pleased to meet the Guru and listen to his wise words.

25

26

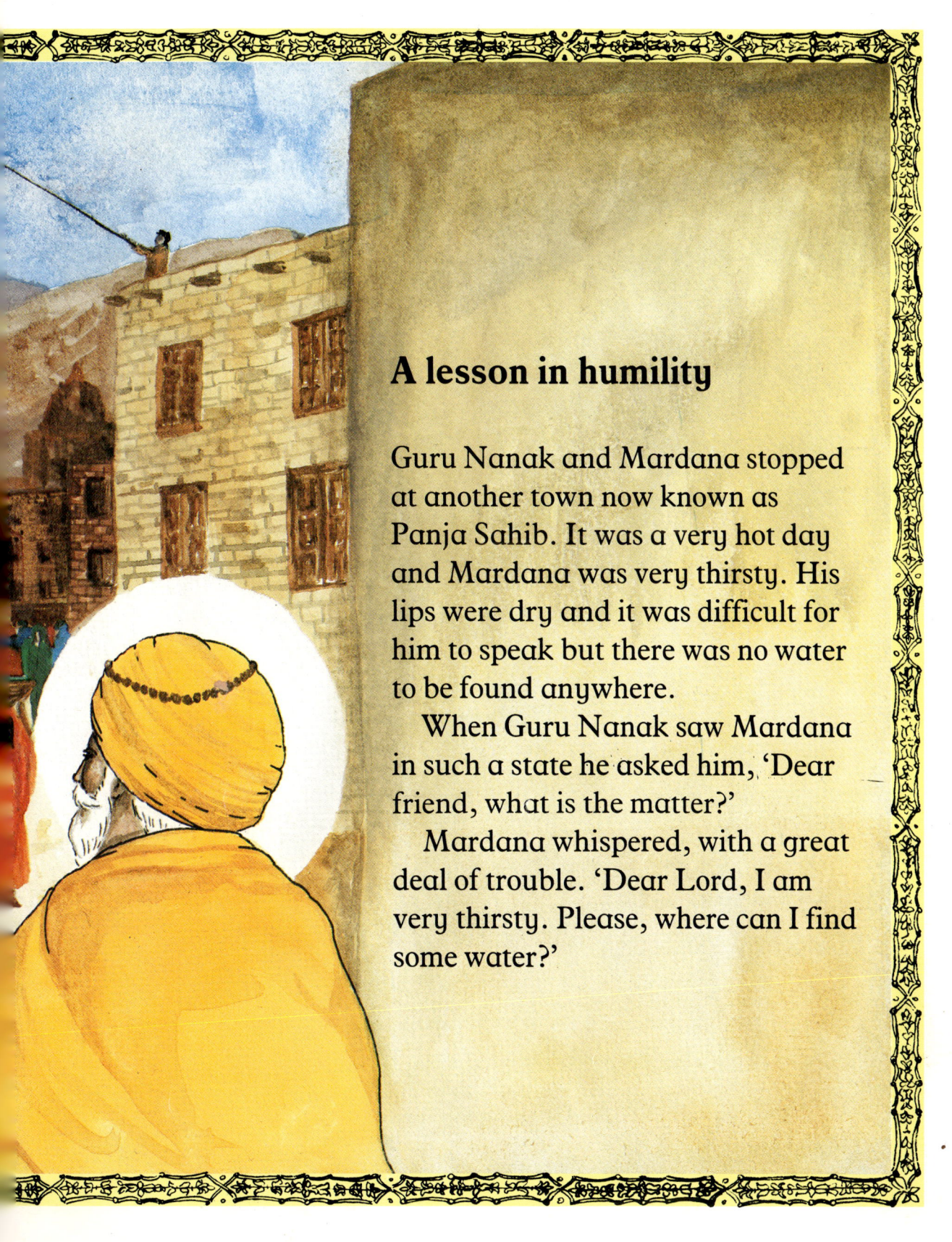

A lesson in humility

Guru Nanak and Mardana stopped at another town now known as Panja Sahib. It was a very hot day and Mardana was very thirsty. His lips were dry and it was difficult for him to speak but there was no water to be found anywhere.

When Guru Nanak saw Mardana in such a state he asked him, 'Dear friend, what is the matter?'

Mardana whispered, with a great deal of trouble. 'Dear Lord, I am very thirsty. Please, where can I find some water?'

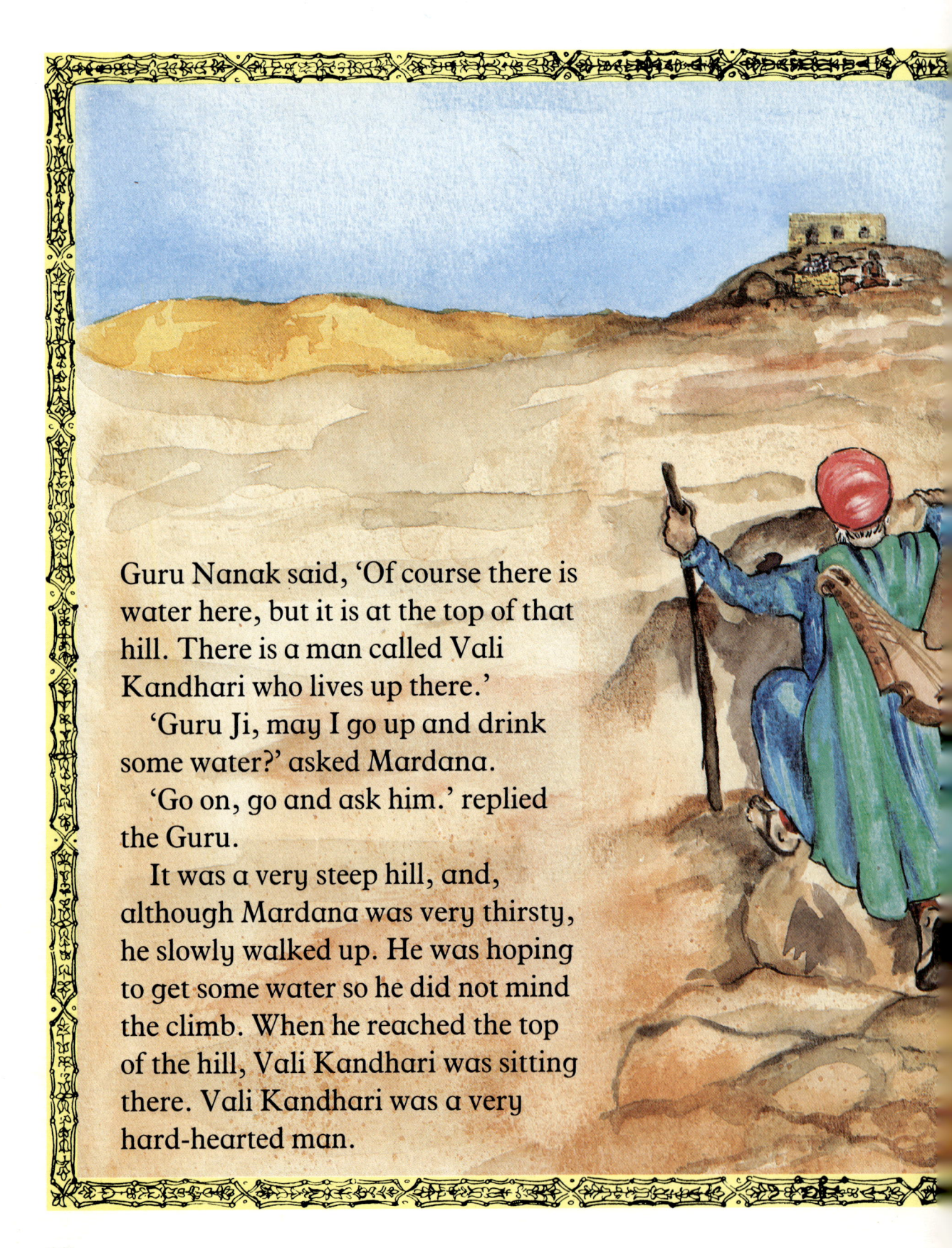

Guru Nanak said, 'Of course there is water here, but it is at the top of that hill. There is a man called Vali Kandhari who lives up there.'

'Guru Ji, may I go up and drink some water?' asked Mardana.

'Go on, go and ask him.' replied the Guru.

It was a very steep hill, and, although Mardana was very thirsty, he slowly walked up. He was hoping to get some water so he did not mind the climb. When he reached the top of the hill, Vali Kandhari was sitting there. Vali Kandhari was a very hard-hearted man.

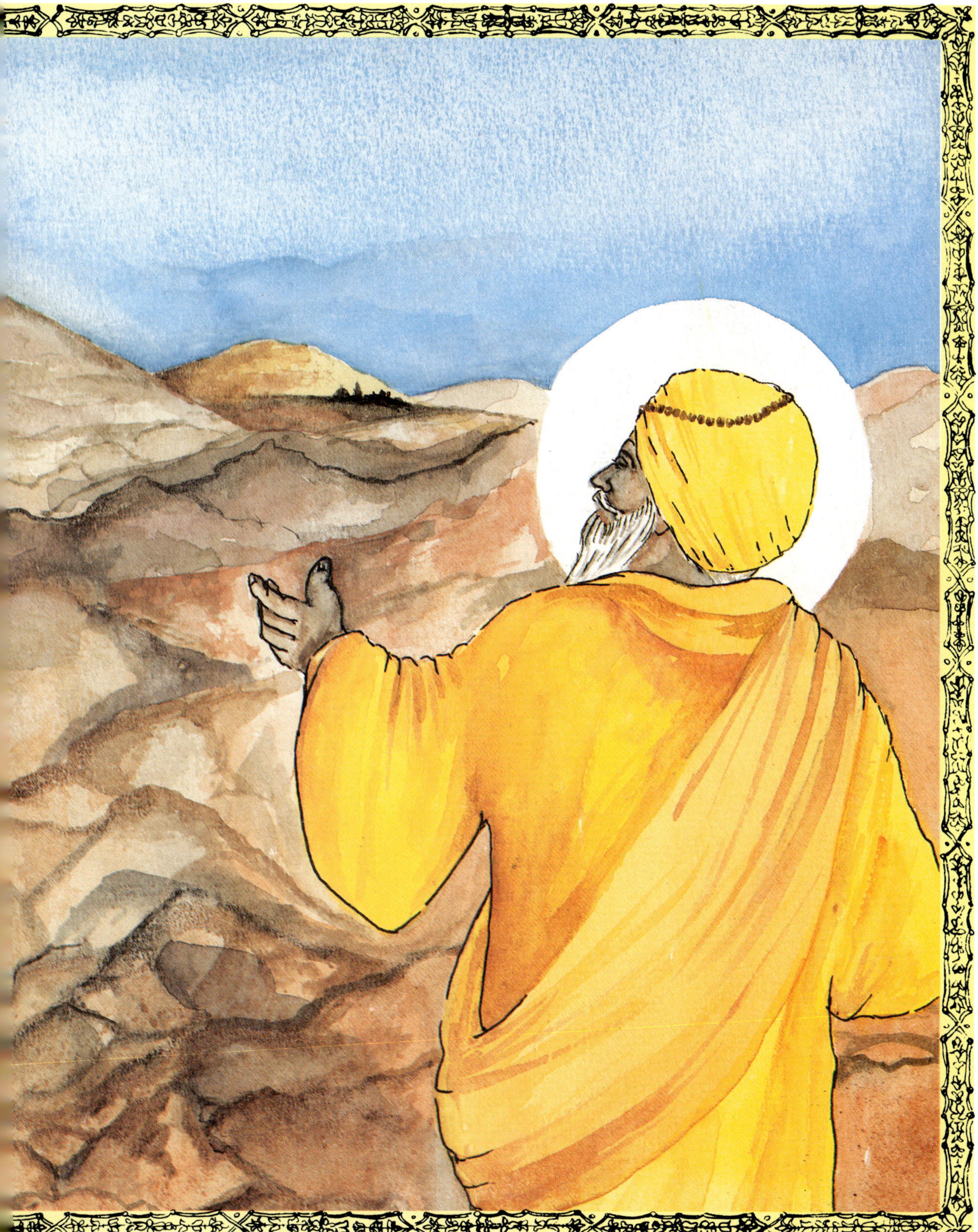

30

'Guru Nanak has sent me' said Mardana 'I am thirsty. Please would you give me some water.'

Vali Kandhari spoke with anger, 'You are a friend of a man who does not believe in my God. Go and ask him to give you water. If he can't give you water, why do you stay with him?'

Mardana begged and begged for water, but Vali Kandhari did not give him any. So Mardana came back more tired and even more thirsty. He told Guru Nanak what had happened.

Guru Nanak said, 'Mardana, go once again. Ask him kindly. Be nice to him. Ask him for water politely. Say to him, 'Won't you please give me some water?'

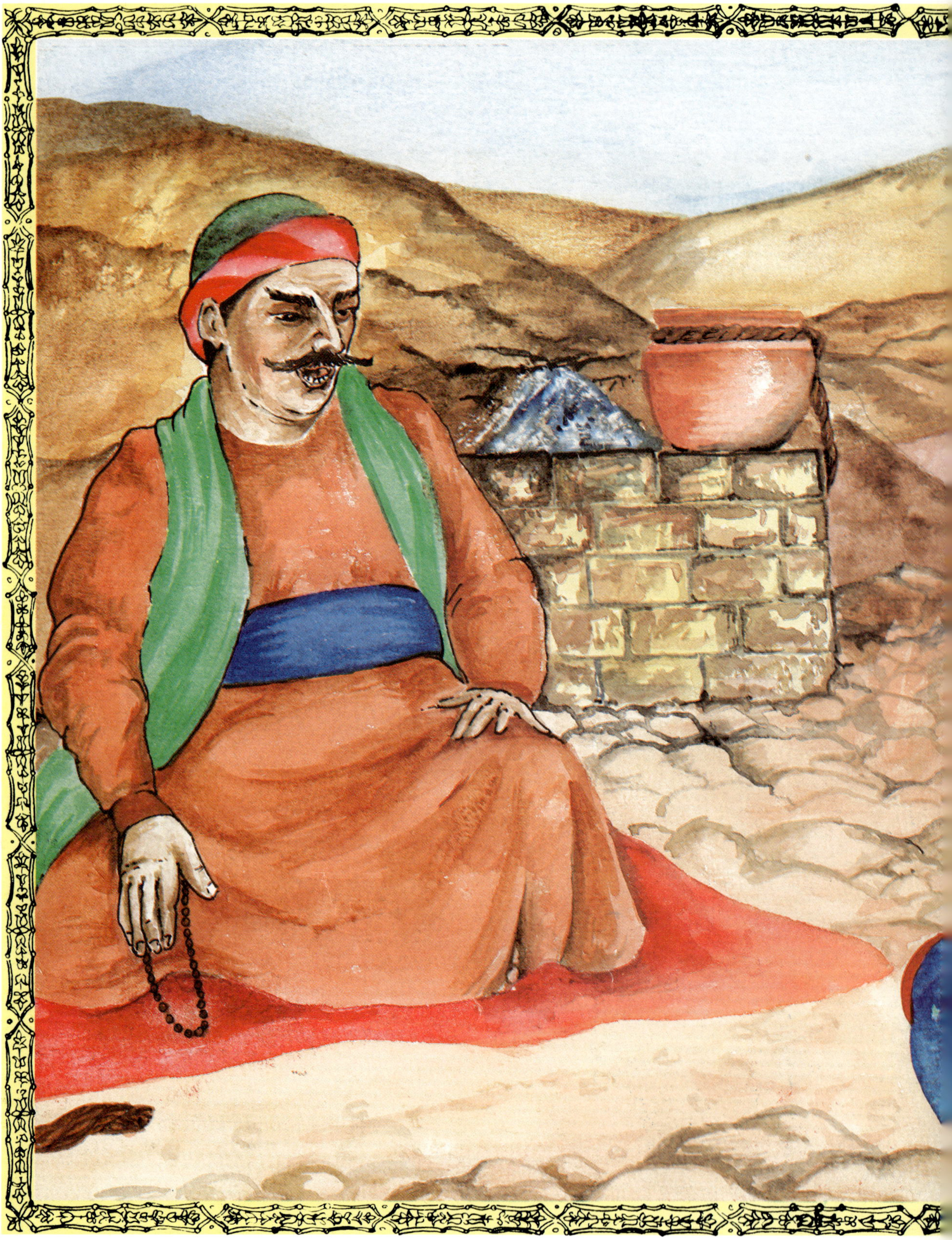

Mardana did not want to go up the hill again, but he had no choice. He was thirsty. So he went up the hill very, very slowly. He then said to Vali Kandhari, 'Please be kind to me. I am thirsty, please give me water.' But again he had to come back without water.

Once again Guru Nanak said, 'Go on Mardana, don't give up now, try once more.'

This time Mardana thought he was going to die. He was so tired and could hardly breathe. He could not stand up straight. But he obeyed the Guru and went up the hill once again. But Vali Kandhari shouted at him, 'Go away, you stupid fool. I am not going to give you any water. This is my hill. Go and get water from somewhere else.'

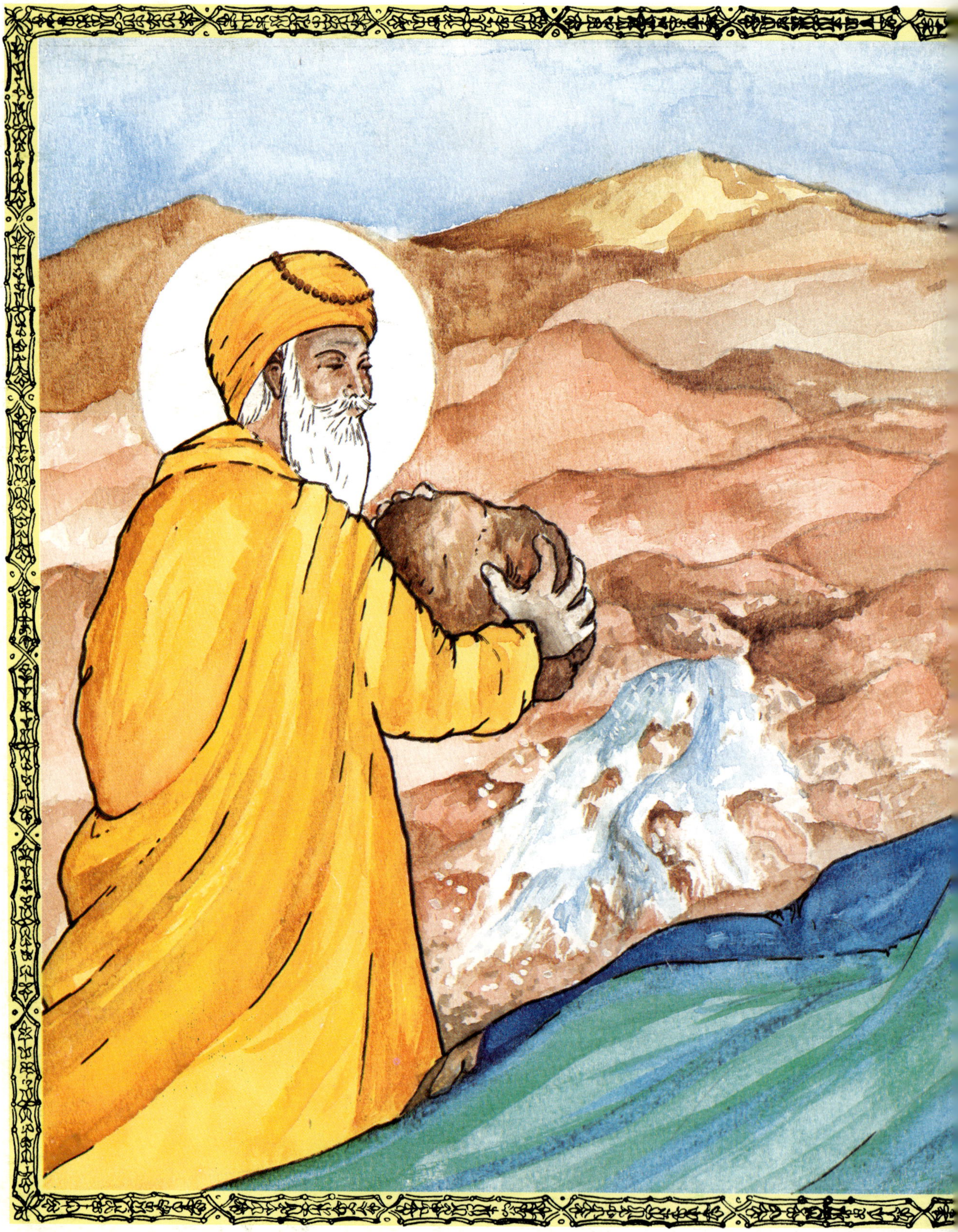

Mardana came back, tired and thirsty. When he got near Guru Nanak he fell down.

Guru Nanak stood up. There was a stone at the foot of the hill which Guru Nanak removed. There was water under the stone and Guru Nanak sprinkled some water on Mardana's face and said, 'Wake up Mardana. Here is water for you.' Mardana got up. He drank a lot of water and felt very happy.

Vali Kandhari was still standing on top of the hill. He saw there was water at the bottom of the hill. He was surprised. When he saw there was no water in his well, he got very angry.

He saw a huge rock and pushed it towards Guru Nanak. He wanted to hurt the Guru. As the rock came tumbling down, Mardana thought, 'Oh dear, I did get some water but this rock is going to kill us.' But Guru Nanak put his hand up and stopped the rock from falling on to him and Mardana. Mardana was very relieved.

At the place where the rock was stopped by the Guru's hand, there was suddenly a beautiful spring of fresh water. A *gurdwara*, which is the name given to Sikh temples, has been built near that place. It is known as Panja Sahib. It reminds the Sikhs that they should be humble.

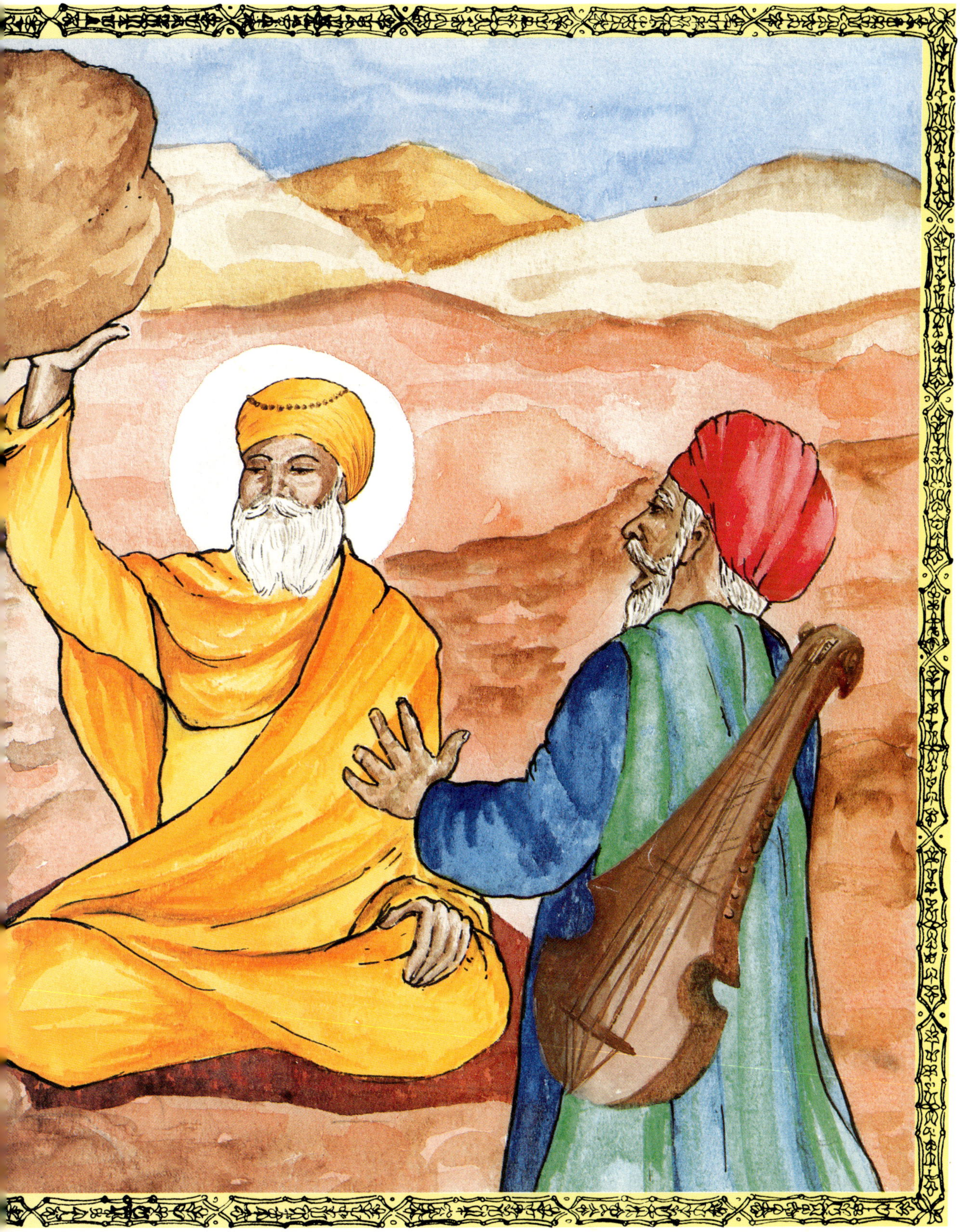

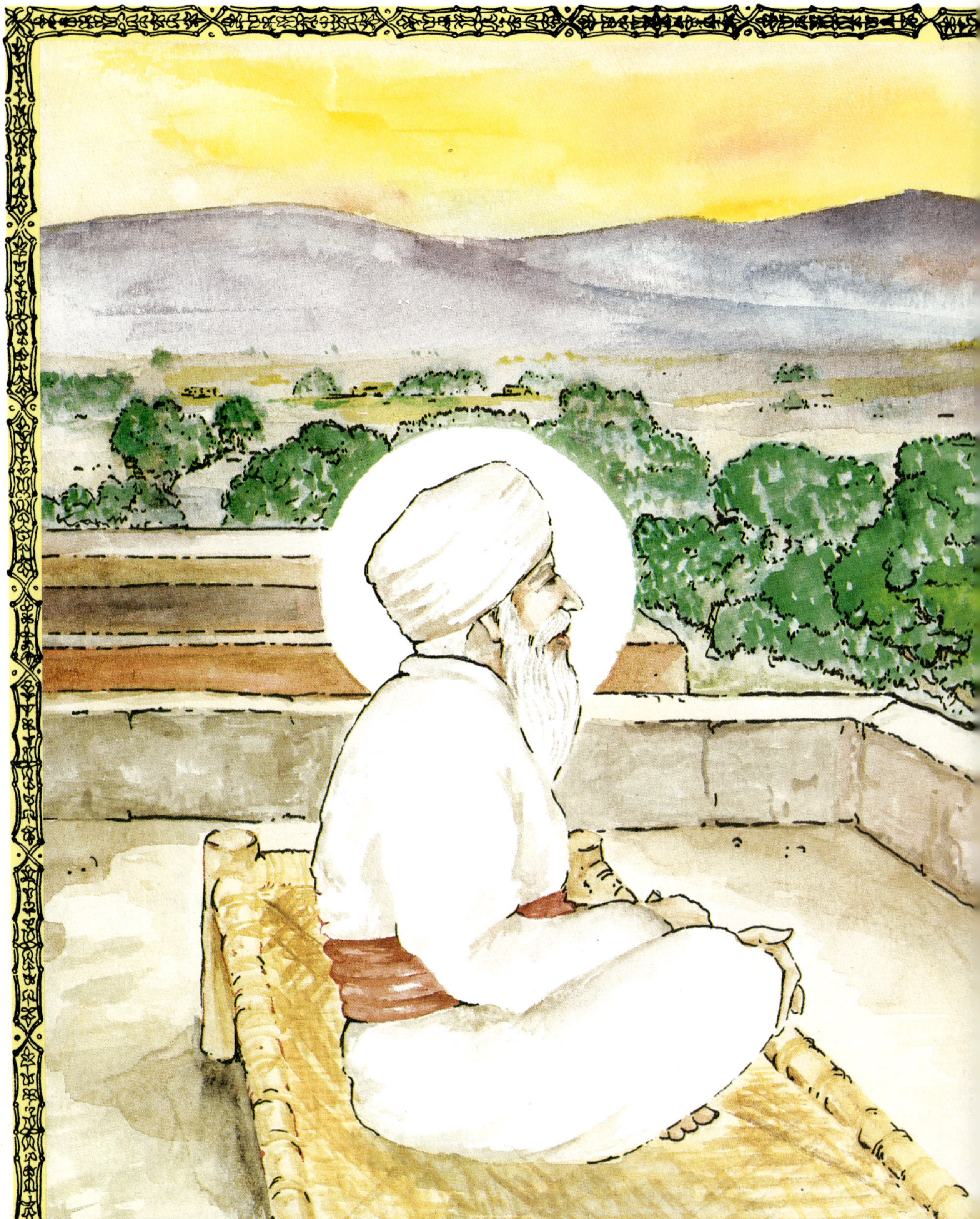

What makes a true Guru

This story is about the third Guru of the Sikhs. Before he became a Guru his name was Sri Amar Das and he lived in a village near Amritsar. He was a shopkeeper. His nephew was married to Bibi Amro who was the daughter of Guru Angad Dev, the second Guru of the Sikhs.

One day, very early in the morning, Sri Amar Das heard Bibi Amro singing Guru Nanak's *shabads*. He liked these songs and sat listening to them for a long time.

When the singing stopped Sri Amar Das asked Bibi Amro, 'Where did you learn to sing so well? Who wrote these *shabads*?' she replied, 'They are Guru Nanak's *shabads*. My father taught me to sing them. My father is very fond of these *shabads*.'

Sri Amar Das said, 'I like these *shabads* very much. Will you teach them to me?'

Bibi Amro agreed to teach the *shabads* to Sri Amar Das. He learnt them all by heart. Then, one day, he said to Bibi Amro, 'I want to meet your father. Please take me to him. I want to become a Sikh.' Bibi Amro took Sri Amar Das to see her father, Guru Angad Dev. The Guru stood up to receive him since they were related by marriage. Sri Amar Das fell at the Guru's feet. He said, 'I am not here as your relative. I have come to be your follower. Please make me a Sikh. Let me serve you.'

Guru Angad Dev was very touched. He helped Sri Amar Das up and embraced him. From then on, Sri Amar Das spent all his time serving the Sikhs who came to visit the Guru but his mind was always fixed on God. He learned by heart all the sacred songs and sang them all the time while he was working.

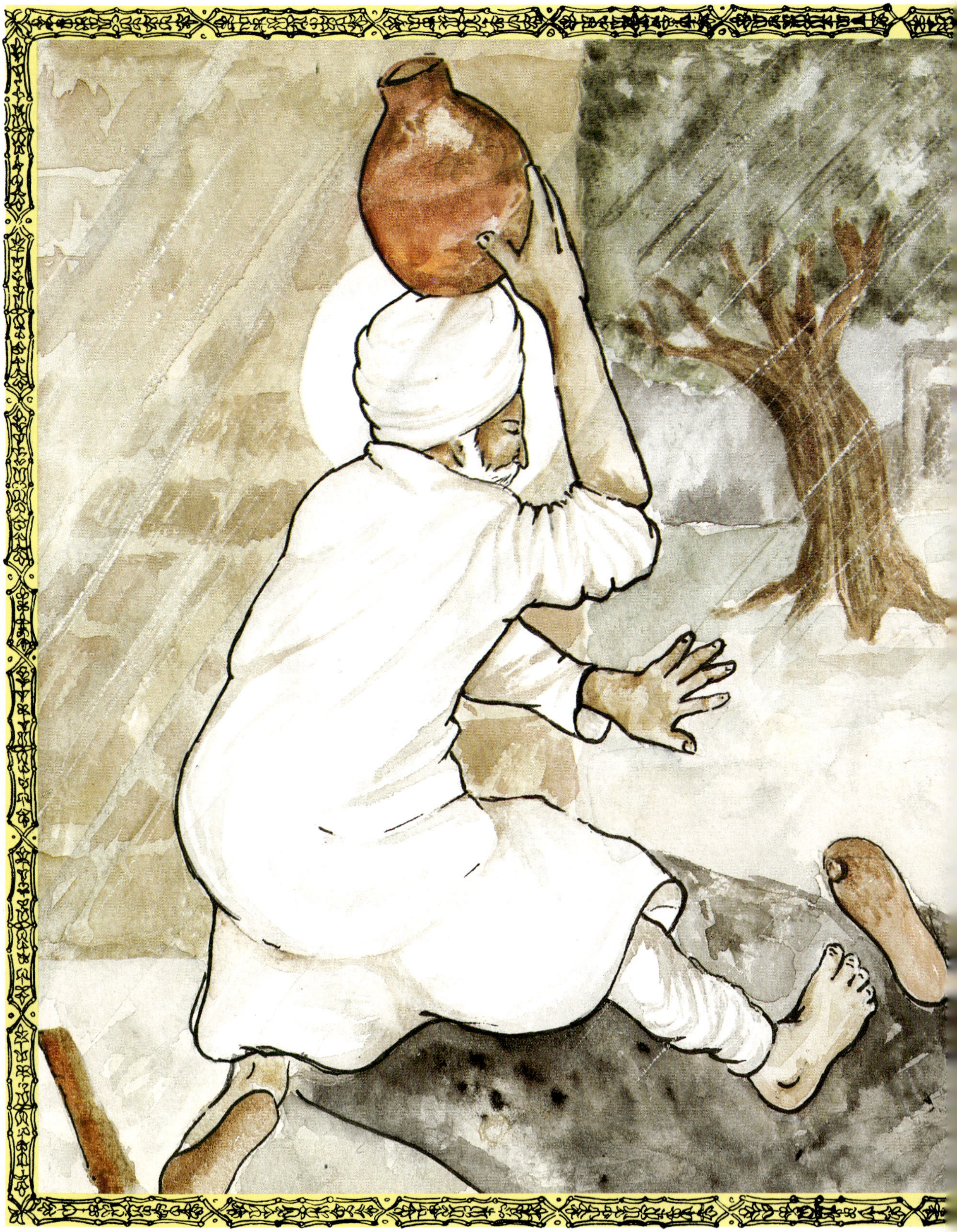

Every day he woke up very early in the morning. He bathed in the river. He brought water from the river for Guru Angad Dev's bath. He never stopped working even in rain, hail or storm. He worked in the *Langar* which is the kitchen attached to the *gurdwara*. He brought water from the well to use in the kitchen. He brought firewood from the forest. He cleaned and washed all the pots.

He worked like that for twelve years. One evening he was walking to the river to fetch water as usual. It began to rain heavily and it was dark. Sri Amar Das reached the river. He filled his pitcher with water and started to walk back. But he lost his way because it was so dark.

There was a weaver's house on the way and his foot was caught by a peg outside the weaver's house. He fell into the hole of the weaver's loom, but he did not let his pitcher fall from his head.

44

The weaver heard the sound and woke up. He said to his wife, 'Someone has fallen into the loom's hole. I wonder who is so mad to go out in this weather?' His wife said, 'It must be the poor homeless Sri Amar Das. He has left his home. He works day and night for the Guru.'

Next day Guru Angad Dev heard what had happened. He did not like anyone calling Sri Amar Das homeless. The Guru said, 'Sri Amar Das is not poor and homeless. He shall be the home for the homeless, the shelter for the unsheltered, the strength for the weak and he will protect those who are in trouble.'

46

Guru Angad Dev then dressed Sri Amar Das in new clothes. He seated him on the Guru's *chawki*, or throne, and placed five coins and a coconut before him. He put a *tilak* on his forehead. Then the Guru bowed before Sri Amar Das and said, 'Sri Amar Das is Guru Amar Das now. He will be the Guru after me.'

The creation of the *Khalsa*

This story is about Guru Gobind Singh who was the tenth Guru of the Sikhs. He was also the last Guru. He created the *Khalsa* which means 'good and pure human beings'. He decided that Sikhs should consider the holy book, the *Guru Granth Sahib*, as the Guru.

On *Baisakhi* day in 1699, Guru Gobind Singh asked all the Sikhs to come to Anandpur Sahib. He was worried that the Moguls were going to destroy the Sikhs. His father, Guru Tegh Bahadur, had been killed by the Moguls. Guru Gobind Singh wanted to make the Sikhs strong and brave. He did not want them to be afraid of death. So on *Baisakhi* day Guru Gobind Singh stood in uniform and fully armed before his people, he said to the Sikhs, 'You need to be strong. You need to fight together. You need to organize yourself as a group.'

49

He then took his sword out of its sheath and said, 'My sword needs a head. Is there anyone in this *sangat* who is willing to offer his head for his Guru? Is there anyone who is willing to offer his head for religion?'

Everyone was silent. No-one moved. They were all scared. After a few minutes, the Guru repeated his demand, 'Is there anyone in this *sangat* who is not afraid to die? Is there anyone who is willing to offer his head for his Guru?'

Still no-one moved. Once again the Guru repeated his demand. Then one man came forward. He said, 'You can take my head. I will give up my life for you.'

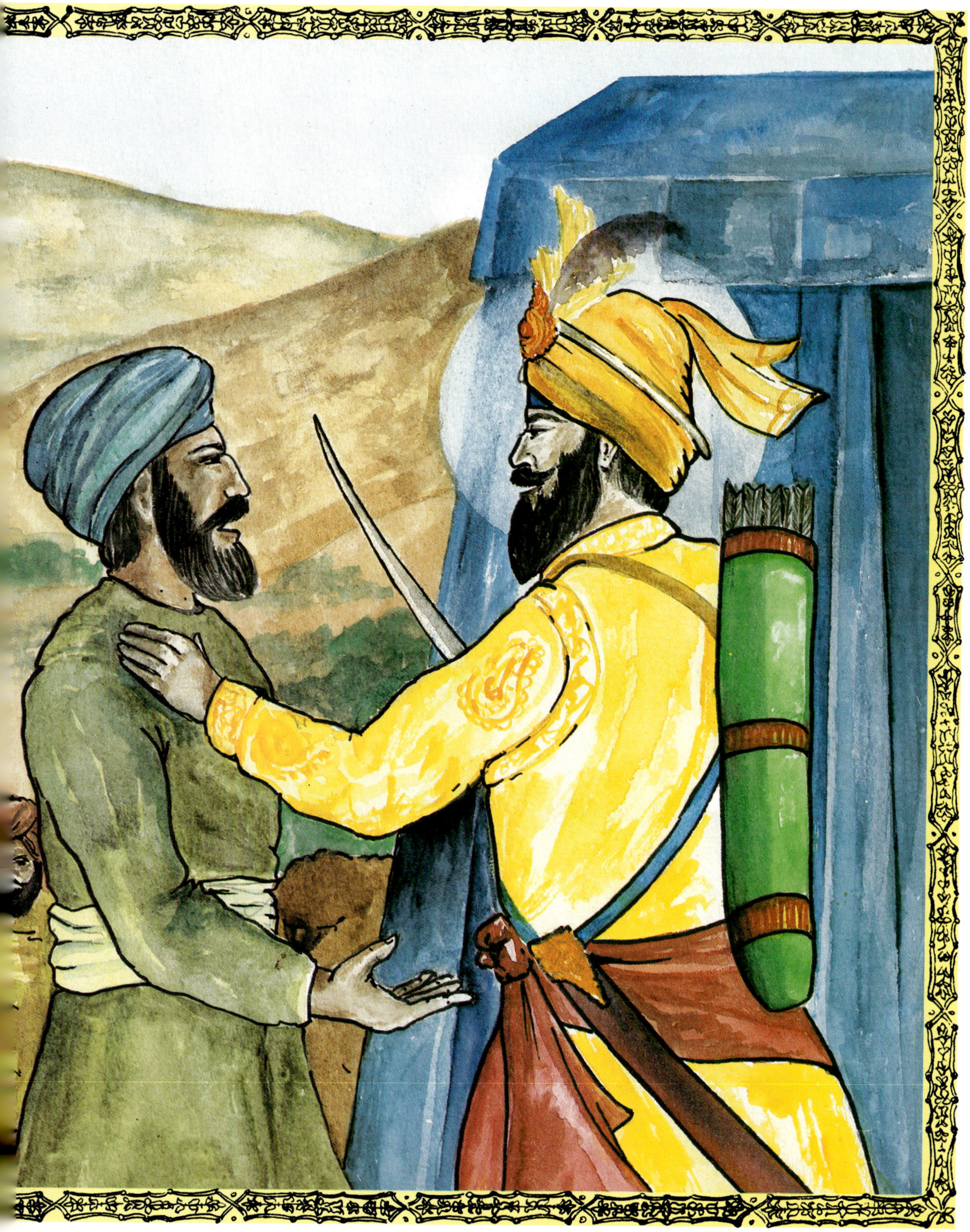

Guru Gobind Singh took him into a tent nearby. There was a loud thud. After a few minutes Guru Gobind Singh came out of the tent. His sword was dripping with blood. He repeated once again, 'My sword needs another head.' Another man came forward. He said, 'You can take my head. I will die for you.'

Once again the Guru went into the tent. Once again he came out with a sword dripping with blood. People began to get worried. Some left the *sangat*. Some said, 'The Guru has gone mad.'

Guru Gobind Singh repeated his demand three more times. Each time the Guru came out of the tent with a sword dripping blood.

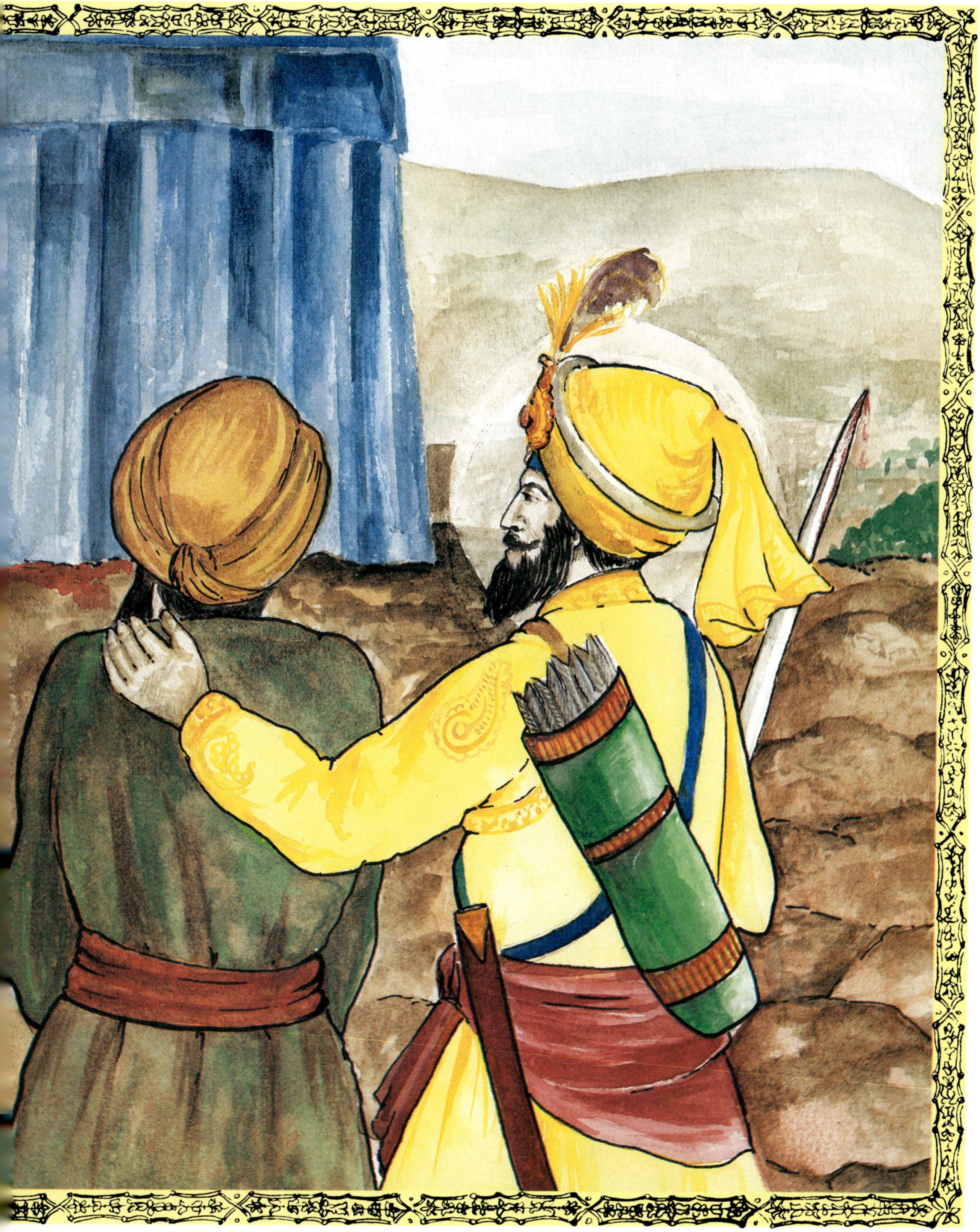

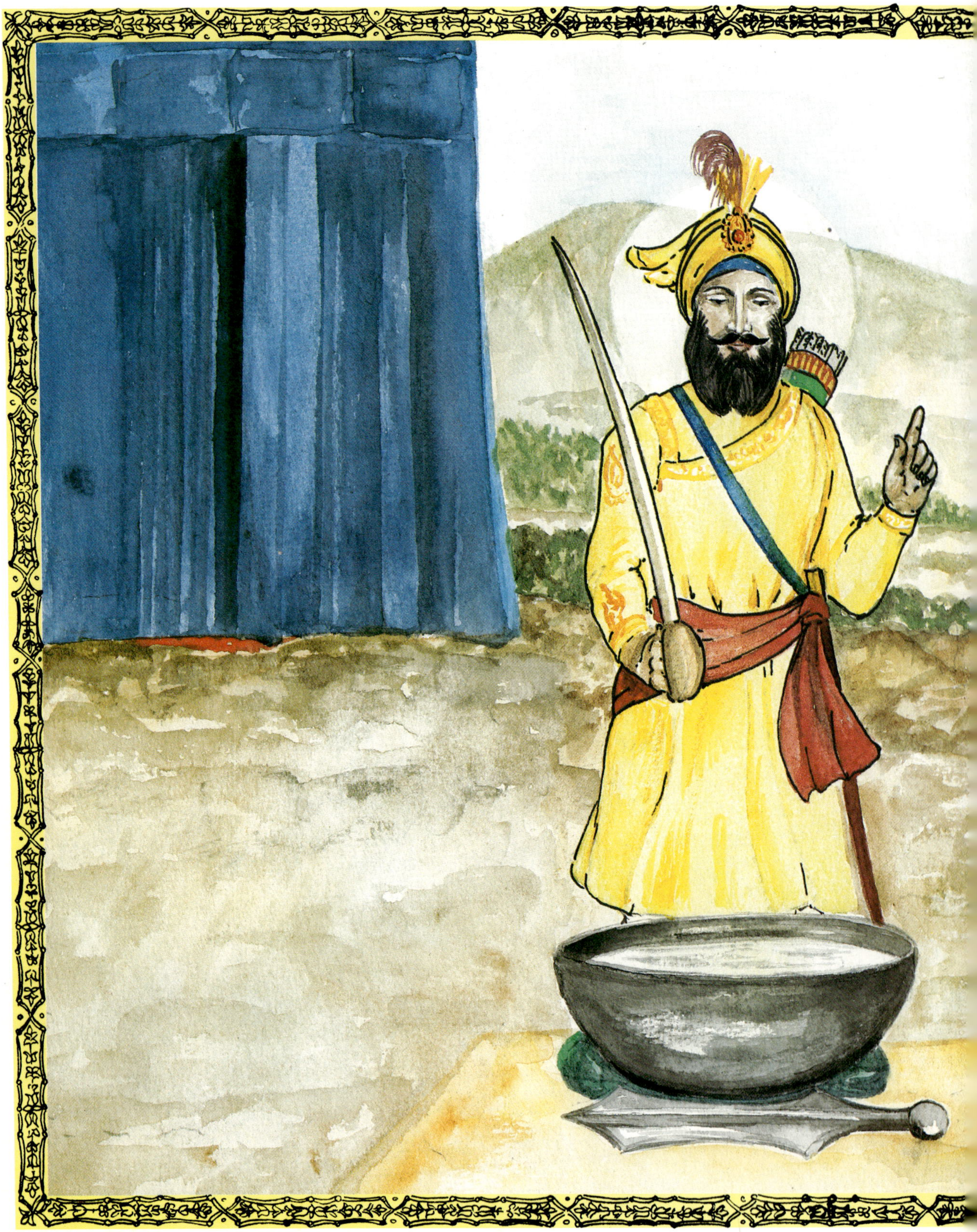

After the fifth man had entered the tent the Guru came out with the five men. They were all dressed in saffron-coloured uniforms, like the uniform worn by the Guru. They were all carrying swords. The Guru called these men 'the immortal five' and *Panj Pyares* (five beloved ones).

He said to the five men, 'My brothers, I have made you the same as I am. There is no difference between us. You have passed my toughest test. You are not afraid to die. You are my five beloved ones. You are chosen by God.'

The people in the *sangat* were very surprised. They were happy that the Guru had not killed these men. The Guru then told the *sangat*, 'These five men are the first five members of the new brotherhood, the *Khalsa*. They are the pure ones. To become a member of the *Khalsa* you have to be brave. You have to be ready to give up your life for the Sikh faith.'

He also told them, 'These five men are of different castes. But they are all brave men. Members of the *Khalsa* must drink *amrit* together from the same bowl. They should all have a common surname. This name should be *Singh* for men and *Kaur* for women.

Guru Gobind Singh made it clear that women can also be members of the *Khalsa*. They can also partake of *Amrit* and be the *Panj Pyares* (five beloved ones).

Guru Gobind Singh then prepared *Khande Ka Amrit*. He put some water and sugar in a steel bowl and stirred it with a double-edged sword. He recited five hymns from the *Guru Granth Sahib*. He then initiated the *Panj Pyares* into the holy order. He asked them to drink *amrit* from the same bowl. This was to make it clear that everyone was equal.

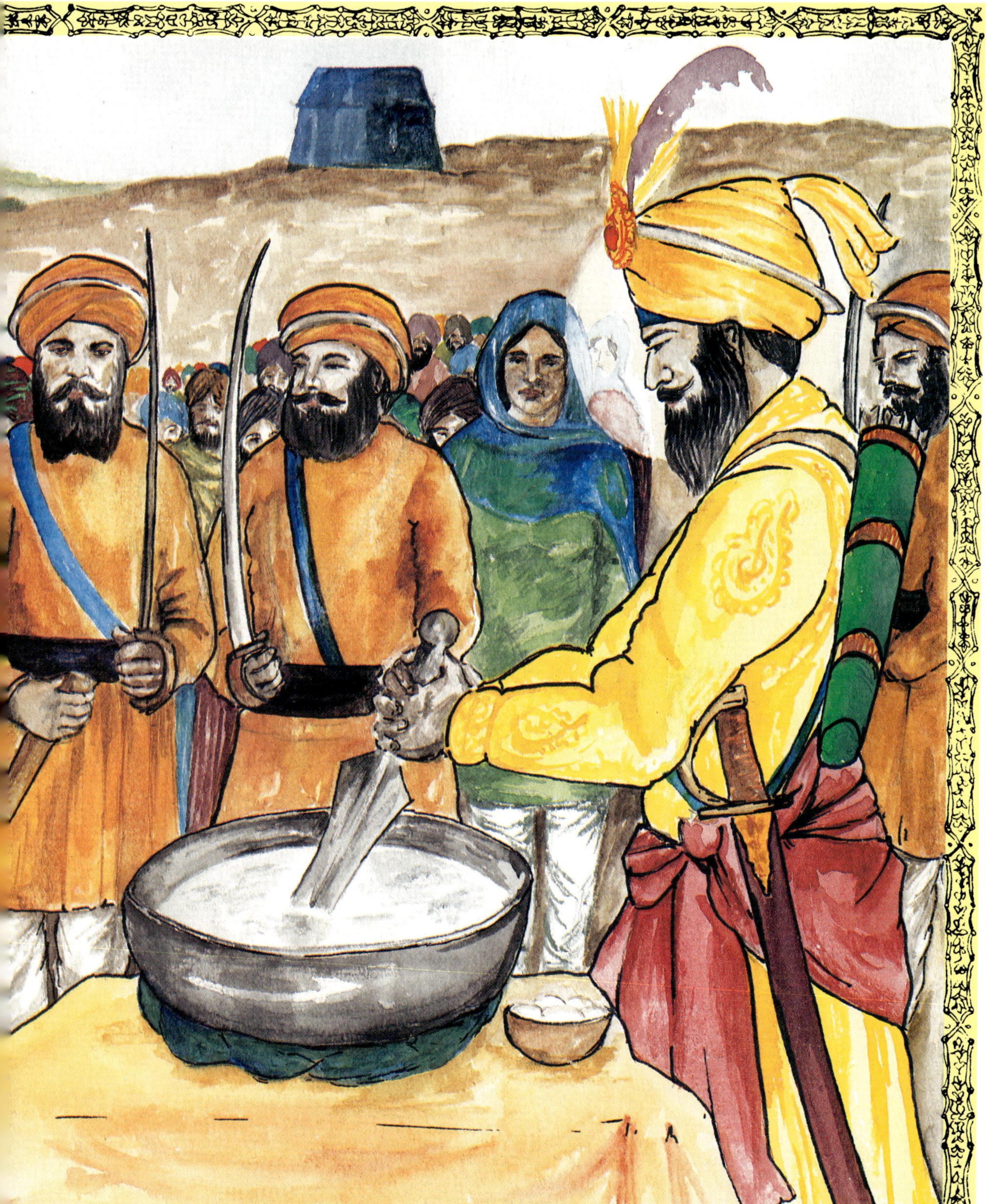

After this the Guru himself took *amrit* from the five beloved ones. This was followed by a ceremony at which large numbers of people were baptized into the Sikh faith.

Ever since that day the *Amrit* ceremony takes place on the *Baisakhi* day. But it can also take place on any other day. Any five people who are members of the *Khalsa* can organize such a ceremony at any time or any place.

Guru Gobind Singh made the Sikhs strong. He removed the fear of death from their hearts. But he was also humble. He himself was the authority and power of *Panj Pyares* (five beloved ones). To this day Sikhs remember Guru Gobind Singh with respect and admiration. They sing his praises as a great man who was a Guru himself but also a disciple of *Panj Pyares*.

Glossary

Amrit The Sikh baptism ceremony. It also refers to a solution of sugar crystals and water used at the initiation ceremony.

Baisakhi day The first day of the Sikh and Hindu New Year. It is celebrated on 13 April. In the Punjab it marks the end of the spring wheat harvest. It also celebrates the founding of the *Khalsa* by Guru Gobind Singh.

Banquet A feast or large ceremonial dinner.

Caste A hereditary class into which a Hindu is born, denoting social status.

Gurdwara Sikh places of worship. The word *gurdwara* means 'House of God'. They are usually built of stone and have four entrances to indicate that they are open to anyone.

Guru Granth Sahib The holy book of the Sikhs which is written in Punjabi verse. The original was compiled by the fifth Guru, Guru Arjun, and was completed in 1604. The Guru Granth Sahib expresses the teaching of all the Sikh Gurus and poets of different faiths. It contains 5,894 hymns and is 1,430 pages long.

Imam A prayer-leader in a mosque.

Kachori A rich type of chapatti (unleavened bread made with butter and wheat flour) which is often stuffed. It is considered to be a food for the rich.

Khalsa Baptized Sikhs. The word means 'pure ones'.

Langar This word means 'free kitchen'. It applies to the kitchens in a *gurdwara* and the food prepared and eaten in it.

Loom A machine for weaving thread into cloth.

Moguls Members of the Muslim dynasty of Indian emperors who ruled India from 1526.

Mosque A Muslim place of worship.

Pitcher A large jug, used mainly for holding water.

Roti A coarse plain type of chapatti usually made with flour and water and is regarded as basic food for the poor.

Sangat A congregation or a gathering of Sikhs in the presence of a Guru.

Shabad The literal meaning in Hindi is 'word'. In the context of the story it is a name given to a religious composition set to music.

Shrine A place of worship dedicated to a holy person.

Tilak A small mark of ceremony made with saffron, a yellow substance obtained from the crocus. Although more popular among Hindu communities, for the Sikhs it is a public declaration of the choice of the individual as a Guru.

Weaver Someone who makes cloth on a loom by crossing threads over and under each other.

Textual note

The Sikh religion, which was founded in 1469 by Guru Nanak, is not a set of views or doctrines but a way of life lived according to a definite model. The personality and teachings of the ten Gurus, as embodied in the 'Guru Granth Sahib', now serve as the guiding force for all Sikhs shaping their careers and their lives.

As a practical religion, Sikhism places great stress on the equality of all human beings. The essence of Sikhism is that people should earn their living by honest means and hard work. It also means that people should share what they have with the poor and the needy. The reason behind such thinking is that you can only love and serve God if you love and serve all the people created by God.

The stories in this book have been chosen to convey messages that cross religious and national boundaries. It is hoped that all children will be able to relate to the underlying moral values that transcend all cultures.

'The story of Makkah', for instance, demonstrates the omnipresence of God. God is everywhere we wish him to be. 'The Banquet of Malak Bhago' is about the values of hard work and honest living which are part of all religions and all cultures. 'What makes a true Guru' conveys two basic messages. One is that Guruship/leadership is not bestowed from father to son. The second message is that anyone who follows the principles of Sikhism is humble and serves others and can earn the respect and title worthy of a Guru. 'A lesson in humility' is a demonstration of God's powers to take from the rich and give to the poor. The last story 'The creation of the *Khalsa*' is perhaps the most significant, through which the concept of equality comes to life.

Additional notes

'The story of Makkah': The Ka'bah is the shrine at the centre of the mosque in Makkah. It is sacred to the Muslims who face it when praying. They consider it offensive to sit with feet facing in the direction of a holy place because feet are thought to be the least clean part of the body as they are in constant contact with the ground.

'A Lesson in humility': Panja Sahib is the famous *gurdwara* built at a place Guru Nanak stopped at during his travels. The rock mentioned in the story, which carries the impression of Guru Nanak's hand, still stands at this place.

'What makes a true Guru': Guru Angad Dev stood up to receive Sri Amar Das because it is customary in Indian culture to stand up to receive a guest and it is also customary to be respectful towards people older than yourself. The 'hole of the weaver's loom' which is referred to in this story, is a big string loop around a wooden peg which is used to secure the weaving loom in the courtyard outside a house. The 'five coins and a coconut' which Guru Angad Dev placed before Sri Amar Das represented the special concerns of a Guru. The coconut symbolizes the universe and the five coins represent the five elements.

'The creation of the *Khalsa*': *Panj Pyare* literally means 'five beloved ones' and refers to the first five Sikhs to be initiated into the new *Khalsa* order by Guru Gobind Singh. The 'five beloved ones' were said to have come from different castes. In Hindu society in those days, these men would not mix socially. Bringing them together and making them his 'five beloved ones', Guru Gobind Singh emphasized the equality of all human beings and removed the distinction of caste from Sikhism.

Books to read

Arora, Ranjit *Sikhism* (Wayland 1986)
Cole, W Owen *A Sikh Family in Britain* (Pergamon 1973)
Cole, W Owen *Thinking about Sikhism* (Lutterworth Educational 1980)
Cole, W Owen and Sambhi, Piara Singh *Meeting Sikhism* (Religious Dimension series) (Longman 1980)
Cole, W Owen and Sambhi, Piara Singh *Sikhism* (Ward Lock 1973)
James, Alan G *Sikh Children in Britain* (Ward Lock Oxford University Press 1974)
Kapoor, Dr Sukhbir Singh *Sikh Festivals* (Wayland 1985)
Kapoor, Dr Sukhbir Singh *Sikhs and Sikhism* (Wayland 1982)
McLeod, W H *The Way of the Sikh* (Hulton 1975)
Singh, Daljit and Smith, Angela *The Sikh World* (Macdonald 1985)
Wylam, P M *A Brief Outline of the Sikh Faith* (Sikh Missionary Society)

For teachers
Cole, W Owen *The Guru in Sikhism* (Darton, Longman and Todd 1982)
Cole, W Owen and Sambhi, Piara Singh *The Sikhs: their religious beliefs and practices* (Routledge and Kegan Paul 1978)

Useful addresses

Sikh Darma Trust UK
Guru Ram Das Ashram
246 Belsize Road
London
NW6

Sikh Cultural society
88 Mollisom Way
Edgeware Road
London
HA8 5QW

Sikh Missionary Society
10 Featherstone Road
Southall
Middlesex
UB2 5AA